SOUND OFF

Spencer Selby

Detour Press

SOUND OFF. Copyright © 1993 by Spencer Selby.
Thanks to the editors of the following magazines and anthology,
where many of these poems have appeared: *Avec* (Cydney
Chadwick), *The Black Warrior Review* (Glenn Mott), *Caliban*
(Lawrence R. Smith), *Grille* (Simon Smith), *Intimacy* (Adam
McKeown), *Lift* (Joseph Torra), *Logodaedalus* (Paul G. Collier),
Long News: In the Short Century (Barbara Henning), *Lower Limit
Speech* (A.L. Neilsen), *Mirage #4/Period(ical)* (Kevin Killian and
Dodie Bellamy), *New American Writing* (Maxine Chernoff and
Paul Hoover), *o•blek* (Peter Gizzi and Connell McGrath), *Painted
Bride Quarterly* (Teresa Leo), *Shearsman* (Tony Frazer), *Situation*
(Mark Wallace), *Sulfur* (Clayton Eshleman), *Talisman* (Edward
Foster), *To* (Seth Frechie and Andrew Mossin), *The Washington
Review* (Joe Ross), and the anthology *The Art of Practice:
Forty-Five Contemporary Poets* (Peter Ganick and Dennis Barone).
This book is dedicated to Gary Sullivan, who gave me an idea.
Published by Detour Press, 1506 Grand Avenue #3, St. Paul,
Minnesota 55105. Distributed by Small Press Distribution, 1814
San Pablo Avenue, Berkeley, California 94702.
ISBN 0-938979-45-0

SOUND OFF

CONTENTS

PENULT

The day I began this work
something curious happened.

There befell the consolation
coming to grips within appearance

of those who leave the light
choice by choice, error by error

likened to battle suddenly hurled out
thru a mouth that prohibits reply.

I came here on the pretext
of relation that confronts something

written in the breach approaching
destruction of imperative control.

For what could never be
I put away the state I hold most dear.

I gave myself over and arrived
at a city where each rampart

became a sacrifice surrendered
on the altar of its untranslated form.

For just one minute I stood frozen
between companions sworn to renounce

the same measure of receptivity
that enabled them to animate

and unify the nameless body
which their offspring now accepted

as their favorite rule of law.
If given half a chance I'd put myself

back there in that company,
with the black pole in the white vortex

whose location is not transmissible
by words grown weary and unappreciative

of my effort to understand the life
held captive behind my current mirror.

I'd speak with all the characters,
observe every function and use

deceptive logic no longer
sounding worried at my expense.

Before you could say good-bye
I'd find myself in immediate touch

with the rupture of presence that brings
a danger I'm unwilling to overcome.

Whenever I think about such scale
my movement spells sabotage

without modifying a single word.
A consequent question stops cold,

thrown back at a hostile audience
when nothing obvious occurs.

A thirst for knowledge denied
between the separate rays of light

illuminating memory wrung from doctrines
of a future I've no time left to avoid.

Believe me when I say I think about
this problem every chance I get.

The light and the dark
the high the middle and the low

won't relieve a distinction
which tosses me back and forth

when I'm standing on a threshold
on the outskirts of original surprise.

That's not the way things happen.
That's not the way at all.

TRACTOR FEED

On the page I've written
how much demanding fortune
always fails to include.

I see a language
which stares down the borders
that build up opinions made over

thru man's propitiated resolve.
The difference I remember
is striking some new obstacle

for the purpose of exploring
blankets spread across the future
colloquial slang or use.

A living aspect must be qualified
by no other reason ground down
upon a context so concrete.

Chance encounters look the wrong way
at my livelihood of work and play
made timely as a subject

in its present alternative role.
Continuity of prejudice
requires antagonism toward my effort

to understand what is happening
with a short-term hammer
that is pounding below my reach.

I say whatever exists is a place
encouraged by words to bring
the end of a quieter day's response.

All knowledge under my discussion
excretes an atmosphere of hunger
in which sober talk is impossible.

I turn my back on various names
that splash their tools and methods
across the endless country

where I teach myself to live.
Construction of my value
shapes a challenge by the minute

that arouses sufficient material
to fill a very large house.
By the time the house is finished

every inch of visible wood
might be commensurate
with one unfamiliar experience.

Each room is quickly surrounded
by the map I've drawn
to give its premise an active design.

Light bulbs in every direction
appreciate twice the usual
pressure applied against my argument.

Black clouds gather in the evening sky.
Bodies fall silent in their foundation.
Experts stop what they are doing

long enough to open both eyes
on the function of a ceiling
now excluded from my system for good.

BATTLE OF THE COVERED SEA

Shadows sometimes die hard.
The so-called projective tests
of personality make use of pictures
which stimulate a subject trapped
beneath the frozen idiom of night.

You walk there where there
is no choice left to resolve.
All modern illustrious candor
structures opinion somehow outgrown
to bring down the status left vacant
by ancient countries that your
thinking hardly ever represents.

Destructive rage thou speakest
lives in the prison-house of logic
you must answer through a
strange allegiance or an
instrumental project held fast
beneath the truth you relegate
to some ruined semblance
of what couldn't happen again.

If limit prescribed a broken rule
then you would be its analogue,
so sculptured to appearance
that the pencil lines it leaves
to block your path shall fare
no better when distracted
from their current job.

Time's loss is an easy thing
to think until actually stated

in a clear-cut encounter
with the evidence above.
A paradoxical word is linked
to nothing quite as lively
as illusion would have you desire.

Say who's hanging around that corner
or you'll have to make the climb
seem hopeless for the rest of the day.
Never enough hands to free
attention and behold directly
what you seek to designate
by works unseen till backed
by specialists many years later,
times hard and times you don't recall
moving in the same direction
just to approximate something more.

Which doesn't mean what it should,
I'm afraid. Not as long as you're
pushing this struggle between two
questions that have one answer
in the middle of your darkest eye.
The music of discovery has brought
you here, but that's not enough.
Starlight pulls at the rope,
shoots another bullet shaped by
memory to examine what it killed.

Both sides open then they close.
It couldn't happen but it did.
Illumination built a fleet
of warships in the desert
that's surrounded by all you see.

The orders are going out:
take no prisoners show no mercy
leave no signs unaltered in the spirit
of their instrumental way.

Like always only more
form figures where you live,
eliminates regalia while it's waiting
for the changes that survive.

LURE

A voice dazzled by light
cannot discern bright objects.

The work it does is a way
to become detached in any case

pushed toward a window growing into
sky and straight-away satisfied clouds

at the start of a venture
that is difficult to describe.

Secret candles of the desert
extract matter from old arrangements.

A certain motive is generated
by disharmony with a certain view.

You string the words you learn
from habit to a hotbed of your fervor.

You come to a number of unasked questions.
You stop and feed this army

with the concept of retaliation
encamped in a huge magnetic field.

At the center of an infinite report
you determine one thing.

All your pertinent company has to go
somewhere more effective than the usual

branch insignia would urge.
Watchdogs cover the earth they resemble,

quicker to set chill breezes
blowing back behind your research.

A blueprint pregnant with necessity
has been inverted across the board.

You see the mind sharing
in the body's experience as if

it were an argument flooded with a light
that blinds your recent advance.

A gap appears in the language
between white and red, doubt

and something absorbed into the skin.
Deep suspicion brings tomorrow

through the high-born spirit
flattened by a cloudless character.

Listen closely from this perspective
spreading across two voices in one.

Walk the path and live for knowledge
that's exasperated by what you see.

Mark the general theme of prayers
you lost through haste to question

every distance you must cover.
Hold the object of your gaze aloft

so both of us can watch it wrestle
with a freedom that doesn't show.

ANXIETY

Anxiety starts in the passage
where a dominant self-made father
spreads his frame of reference
across a desert with no plants.

For miles in every direction
a uniform canvas stirs not.
Confusion as to what will occur
makes a high-pitched sound

your only opening accepted
and moving toward the light
you know is there to draw
a spitting image from its home.

Sky toward downward view
changes color as it tightens
all the fingers holding
verbal understanding at bay.

No one present will recognize
early significant experience
that stands outside the wellsprings
of this present work.

Preemptive though it be,
the vast expanse gained notice
enough in stories almost forgotten
when their circumstance is glorified

under orders from somewhere else.
No amount of formal armour
can prevent exaggeration
of the battle yet to come.

Your method spells madness
in a blind attempt to leverage
the weaker position resting
carefully behind your mouth.

Sudden waves of meaning
drive back the future rhythmic
desire which holds you fast
inside two powers for the purpose

of challenging anonymous delay.
Crossing over so much data
does speak the uprush
called to judgment from above.

Tempest by punctual rule,
damage smitten full at last,
corrective nature uninfluenced
unto hearing once loved names

that now would blacken
every pleasant sounding eye.

EXPOSURE

The world's night
is spreading stolen boundaries
from one attachment to another.
Streets I have never walked,
houses I have never seen,
come out of my mouth
like a question mark.

A brave soldier
has decided not to accept
the old way of balanced forces
until my answer is assured.
The card before me is either the ace
or the deuce of spades.
Both will guess
and both will make their judgments
lucky to be wrong.

Conviction walks the plank,
splits you up the middle,
drops your side in disagreement
by providing rituals in which
the highest ceiling is omitted.

Nothing from your memory
remains outside an object
where awareness is impossible
to reason with.
Like a child absorbed in his toy
the clear sky is drawn too close;
identity is more improbable
than what is brought forth

through the words you know as perfect
and so appealing when they're far away.

A separate nucleus below
encounters difficulty in fusing
the flesh of expectation
to your former name.
A weight is pulling against the drapes
in a big room lashed against the process
you should never think about.

Tension you can't verbalize
fills up the night,
determines another circumstance
in answer to the charge
of embezzlement of knowledge
that made you lie and scheme
and beg for more.

Your downfall has a limit
but exposure has none.
All the splendid darkness
must disregard experience
on grounds you cannot show.

Memory takes its time
with that burden of development
which it doesn't recall.
Before long something flashes
in the corner,
lifting up the tablet that faces action
by arresting each opponent
without containing material ignorance.

I'm sorry I had to turn you in.
I promise not to reveal the secret
of our conflict during waking hours,
when your beauty and your meaning
are so widely out of view.

As long as I have breath
I'll always defend this space,
and you can be my promise unfulfilled.

LIVID

Brainwashed for centuries
would become a choice.

Possible impossible or what
attachment you are after

when wanting to expose a meaning
that is outdated and useless.

A tremendous molecular pressure
is built up that can only

result in shameless company
encompassing your route.

The terrible preemptive shadow
you have before you

shall not be recognized as such
by these or any associates.

To drink up paradox
through your own volition

is negated in whatever
you might transmit to another.

Just knowing what to do
is insufficient.

Where knowledge so strips
memory, none will answer.

The sins of momentum have been
desensitized within the framework

of opposites which pass through
the mirror of your reflected form.

The more you seem to know
about yourself, the more power

there is in certainty
of what you don't accomplish

while you're pushing
for something tremendous.

Between one struggle too many
and a headlong fall, there can

only be impatience with the logic
of your greatest surviving goal.

You can't take things as they are
when you're yearning to experience

what might be totally worthless
from another perspective.

Maybe that's why one word
says it all so often.

One line one sentence
starting stopping something

carried from one edge to the other
without ever leaving home.

THE LONG DEFAULT

Words make sense
written slowly in a message
placed before observant eyes,
eyes I don't remember at their birth.

The chance I left is moving
underneath chromatic paint,
vanishing once it's full of profit,
similar to voices
that will never think of home.

Exception led astray
would stop and show its hand
at the smallest excuse,
neither opposing content
nor swallowing anything
assuming your response.

I think I dared to call you
on your simple property;
you don't own it
but it's yours nonetheless.

Can I enter?
will you give me my best example
pushed back into darkness
at the service of your only heart?

My proposal like my vision
makes you smile and then approach
the unspeakable sentence
more terrible and more dreamlike

when sticking to a subject
that we both agreed was wrong.

Rising murmurs
either neutral or averse
adopt a name you recognize
on both sides of an office
where we meet and curb
an appetite so true.

Old burden same fate
as yesterday moving further
and further outside judgments
not exactly understood.

Rock built earth,
trees and plants and creatures
of memory building up weapons
for a struggle that is sitting
on your head, playing out
a scene you won't easily forget.

One tough looking truth
is ready to show itself
why the blame we shared didn't work.

Trouble in a different time
shall spread each verbal accident
across the streets we walk alone,
shall read the news so lost in life
of reasons we're not able to avoid.

Maybe that's the way it works
when someone aggravates a feeling

of knowledge betrayed,
starting over with experience
bound by old and new alike.

Can you tell the difference?
does my fable call you strongly
to order bearing the sharpest
division more often than not?

Odd sound, chief circle,
timeless structure pressing
down upon a way of life
not verified until it's too late.

Regardless of the method used
I always come back to your door;
I knock three times
and then I fall asleep.

Signs are everywhere
but they don't mean anything
as long as we're apart.

UNWRITTEN LAW

The world of writing
won't give you what you want.
You ask, it answers,
"I can't be had."

You read on different levels
that one must perceive reaction
put in sequence to set aside
delivery of letters so furious
as to be a most effective tool
for only half the work.

Treatment begins with the mouth open
and the teeth exposed.
Each blade is brought in quickly,
picked up by the tongue
and then the moment of truth arrives.

A buzz-like sound is unanchored.
Memory vanishes and reappears
under conditions more typical
and more inviolate than before.

There is no present
you might then write
as shorthand entertaining
a force in the world
most recently destroyed.

You sense what God had mentioned
falling in between predicting
which avoidance shall never be repaired.
You look upon a clock to find

the name for beauty in consort
with each terrible demand.

The hand wanders, gives up
a situation no one told you to oppose.
Your lips are locked on something
clumsy and powerless,
something written when all urge to escape
leaves you utterly alone.

Satisfied, that's what you are
when passing over ruined country
known so well since birth.
Your logic deserves a crime
driven out into the world
of self-interest and passion
and infinite annulment of a question
you cannot survive.

Silence of a heart
you are always measuring
stoops a little too far
in the aftermath of no immediate
payoff or response.
Negative slumber braves the opposite
predilection torn from darkness
more defensive all the time.

Shadows fall and close your eyes
in language both material
and appropriate to many symptoms
of producing feeling
that's now even unto itself
an entity withdrawn.

Escape might not be worth the pardon
granted in the interval surrounding
anything you choose to associate
with delivery of the current blow.
Timing not expected
makes a mockery of spirit
divorced from atmosphere of license
in your better cries for help.

Old charges worship readings
which you then betray.
Bad taste is removed
before it gets a chance to work.

Secret police look you in the eye
outside of memories huddled together
at the level of an unwritten law.

NO WAY

There's no way to stop that trouble
we thought would put us in the middle

of some dark prophetic circle
fueled by the breath of another extreme.

No way to see through objects
which depend on repose of reconcilement.

No way to format perpetual wakefulness
from dictums of needful analysis.

No way to satiate hunger only interested
in maintaining its own continuity.

No way to wipe out blind acceptance
of secondhand arguments.

Go on, acknowledge what you can't do
where you can't go, then perhaps

the broken intensified force comes back
for more than you might rectify.

Bitterly appreciates dissuasion
of unmanned conflict of frost and fire.

Willing almost to assume some helpful
twist of greater proportion beyond all

nurturing style that still must keep us
in its grasp for as long as possible,

hoping that the routine circumstance
we live for will never have an end.

And why not, and why else follow
what you need to blow yourself up

with selfish negations you can't
find or contemplate any other way.

Each guilty harbor comes and goes
with or without awareness turned up

in silence soon mistaken for the whiteness
of a cloud, the image passed on daily

from one mirror to another. A question
with no answer penetrates the sky,

upsetting as always the chemical balance
which you worked all day to preserve.

It seems you are lost in a jungle
displayed through every sign of life that

you can't get your hands on, closing in
then falling back when probability says

it just wants a good honest watershed
with which to ride things out.

LEFT TO OWN ENDS

That devil was left to his own ends.
All day long hard drop of darkness

came up thru the floor and raised
each question too tireless for words.

Every risk brought knowledge that
he wasn't really qualified to bear.

One kind of illusion and another
kind of clifftop saved by curious

language trapped inside a memory
made impossible by his descent.

One drop too many and there he was,
a stranger with a wild career

crossing solitude made counterfeit
by thoughtfulness and dread.

Fingertips let no shadow fall
more flagrantly than just that

very epilogue made up in advance.
Discovery all the more convenient

for its crooked sense of truth—
a sense by which all people seek

to purify the limits of forgetfulness
that desecrate their earth.

And soon enough they're wrong
and sure enough they'll stop

right there in the undergrowth
and prove this isn't the case.

They'll smile and argue
and activate a voice in the desert

moving forward toward rebellion
but it won't be enough.

Left to their own ends before
they are aware, ominous as windows

blurred by meanings closed to any
other embrace that they might enjoy.

Gone full circle with convictions
not extinguished by a painless death.

Rigid splendor carved from habit
in the best and worst society alive.

The only one we've got,
that's what they like to say

when every argument is done
and all the words drop off

toward knowledge that is sure
enough replaced by something more.

UNDER THE GUN

For L. O'Meara

At once explosive and unknown
the lines I write are true

but only in the interstice
that forms when given

another excuse to advertise
a remedy I no longer apprehend.

Things motivating this channel
erect a structure that houses

a classroom called to order
in an ancient pit where every

subject must fail every test
and forget every answer

but one that never seems
to matter when it counts.

Two people meet in the corridor
and exchange notes late at night

and twenty years later
their impossible interplay

brings down the house.
Between outside and inside

plus minus difference
reestablished like a valley

that follows the present
there is nothing but disaster

currently observed
or articulated somewhere else.

Whenever danger threatens
underground agencies are formed

against the chance made manifest
to quiet heart and mind

and receive the benefit of X-ray
burns confined to one dedicated

expert witness gazing out across
a neighborhood in love with doubt.

All meaning that is not absorbed
will take to the other side and

treat each new danger as a joke.
The solitude thus encountered

can't really see enough to guide
this experience from its source.

And so behold the time struck
dumb from lack of alternatives.

Double up a modern precedent
beyond all expectation of material

that got us here and won't
let us go without a fight.

Take up arms against a day
known or recognized from other

experiments projected ahead
in the discharge of any antidote

kept out of reach and removed
from present awareness

for the good of all these
relationships under the gun.

THE LOCK

Do not look too closely
at postmodern damage
repeatedly found in advance
of a claim you sometimes find
in dreams benumbed by the icy shaft
of future neighborhood fear.

Sad coherence of a day
which each of us
incessantly call our own.
Morning after morning
starting in the wrong space
no longer filled to a limit
that permits differences
beyond our power to finally let go.

One viewpoint twice saved
and five times backed against a wall
would not be enough,
would not move the house to tears
or tear it down and build it back up
without examining its own
version of an accident
doing most ancient work
in the fewest words possible,
sticking a knife in your throat
where it hurts the most
but won't be felt by anyone
who might have a very different
attitude to bear.

That would be too easy;
that would be one statement

too many propped up in a story
we can never assimilate for long.
Insurgent forms collapse
each time such abandon shows what
presence failed that of the living.
Changing schemes gain nothing
serious dominated by powers
of earth and sky attached
by a string to the moment
when we really become old.

One way or the other that's trouble
just now getting in the know,
findings recognized where nothing
typical seems to show,
perverted light sent back
thru a long length of bridgework
hoisted over a wall
tortured imprisoned starved to death
and then left to fend for itself
until something is written down
containing a nerve leading out
across the perimeter of things
resisted and diminished
and argued about long after
the present geography is gone.

PLATFORM

It would be better if I could remember
the difficult challenge stuck in a time
recounted beyond all relevant delay.

Likelihood and defiance
shining outward across the blackness
which no reason ever illustrates.

False start forced to remain silent
while your fingers excite sensory motions,
pull back lines of the second window's

desire to win paradise from unjust effort
you remember in coincidence replayed now
as if its warmth emanates from other

voices lighting up the unprotected grave.
And can't that mean I love you
as a world I can melt away as costly

indulgence of all sides added together
at the very moment stepping outside
history bangs and hammers on your head.

Don't you drive that message thru a limit
groping for unnumbered centuries,
beloved of itself in classic metaphor,

told with a truth not saved anywhere,
pushed aside by language
which no narrative shall ever forgive.

Another version of the same story
would leave your answer baffled
by being thrown into a glare of light

stuck between a line and a point
indifferent to its rescue
and certified destructive either way.

This logic so pleased your forecast
that now all memory must dote on pleasure
turned visibly to sickness at the end.

Admission by whom all other thoughts
are mingled with their host, danger
from where each circle gets its blood,

stop thy judgment with the deepest powers
you can muster, make the dead from
living passage struggle to withdraw.

Walk right out over and above
a platform which you never believe
should stand on the evidence alone.

ANTHEM

Before writing is a movement
that rejects your designation
surrounded by a white halo
emerging from an open tree.

A small branch sticks out
by degrees prolonged in darkness
after too much effort
poring over unfixed meanings

with a cross to indicate
the rupture of original intent.
We stand on common ground
remembered for one shifting voice

rather than two lines harmonized
to effect some chicanery
that bad money and lost belongings
both would call their own.

We'll execute that contract
if it kills us
when a symptom we are showing
falls conveniently asleep.

Can't tell whether by choice
or through necessity
the hand suddenly clenches
and reaches up in the air.

The urge to grasp articulated sounds
tracks down knowledge stuffed
with useless tactics, virtue, memory,
halting the interminable work.

Certain music has lit a candle
in the forest known by some
as mere adornment within desire,
beyond all thought.

No reasoning will help endow
a sentence not admitted or attuned
when hastening the perplexity
of such an injurious approach.

To phrase a more inventive choice
life outside beginning
is now divided
beneath the limit of six directions.

The first three succeeded
in changing people's hearts
for good and for bad at once.
Substantial ground rose up

and returned to obligation
which would undertake the whole
of the work involved in building
an entrance into the next.

Figures of the order we can't recall
did strip the error-freighted concept
now retained in numbers faces
exposed to the moon.

Who knew and suddenly remembered
they would get there first?
Who proceeded on the chance
ruined every time they're out in front?

The same group gets very nervous,
says you'll owe us nothing
if you lose your best kept
secrets along the way.

Movement becomes an outline
headed toward the center,
trapped by its agenda
on a newly erected wall.

A face carved or covered in suspicion,
a prisoner of useless data
stuck right here in memory
until it proves itself unwilling

to operate through dreams
we might be better off without.

ROUGH TONGUE

for R. and K. Waldrop

No language native in a pair of lips
still fresh with heat of attention
that my mind has foreseen most carefully
to yield a Basic English
burned away by its own curving pride.

Memories of waiting open the present,
gliding outside getting out
beyond a statement whose fibre
doesn't rub us differently.
Reflex complicated by desire
is not my point of a failed liveliness.
The window of night before and after
a simple interior engulfs direction
whose eye is a myth I remember
in time for phenomena I cannot deceive.

A word empties its story
nailed to the spot through whom
there isn't an artful backward glance
made of orders cleared to reveal
performance diverted from the day before.
Nothing has happened as very useful
for that internal garden
that you never knew you said.
Fragments of a skull have to be covered
in the message that still takes you
through a season without reward.

Puzzles break and break down
like rivers you forget in the rain.

You live on the surface of second hand
shadow stones so brightly diffused.
A value appears only when falling asleep
with gunfire sounding directly above your head.
Pressure precedes relief
used as curtains to resist acculturation
of knowledge named after an echo
reverberating across the possible areas
in which a figure speaks of limit
in order to walk away like a quivering animal
duped by the curve of its latest revenge.

If only Providence could shift her attention
to the moment this libertine wears tomorrow
as a large ambiguous umbrella
sold everywhere for free.

That is what I say and what I am,
hand and mouth gesturing without renouncing
an unearned matter of the first importance.
Can't take away camouflage for concrete
life signs variable in an optic
perspective or object
surrounding substitutes as per agreement
of the anecdotes that laugh at any certain death.
Won't choose between all these cannibal
spirits of conclusion which devour
one another like a line of mountains
at the window where it hurts.

Such honesty is not what I accommodate
to drain the sound of honeyed words
imbued with movement that my language
has intentionally absorbed.

Sunlight isn't the only answer
which prolongs a formulation for advice
called into question
from beneath a simple sentence
locking out this body at its dark unwinding skin.

LEGACY

Darkness rules by something prior
to one's given procedure, focus or delay.

Extensive straightforward meaning
goes funny before it's written
in the face of impending disaster.
Fire we have to drink
sees water in its late arrival.
Newly offered machinery
turns chance back upon a wilderness
which reads that stupefaction
as an unavoidable response
to something we don't ever want to say.

In times left out we dream and sleep
with body focus of reality fashioned
by ground swells of surface momentum.
Accumulated reactions exhibit
the spinal column's way
of protecting itself from things
prior to each unrelenting
judgment that we make.

The essence of digits feared
and then broken down, the fruit
of labor shaken by humans
not present outside of everyday life;
these payments and more
are what we have taken in exchange
for streets and vehicles intersected
by routes we never allowed to exist.

Behind the logic settling over
all we're left with, this urge to write
an answer has come and gone.
Interference of the body
pressed hard against experience
takes improbable words
with a pigmented something
breaking its attachment
to an old-fashioned laboratory window.

Total problematical assault
is now dividing up coded messages
that our camera smashed
against the rocks below.
A succession of flashes moves outward
from the center of a conflict
we thought we had left behind.

At the top of a highway looming ahead,
crossed and recrossed by flesh
rinsed with water and pain,
we take the pages we have written
toward some miracle forgotten
by age-old products that tell us
where to belong.

We take what we are given
and then we decide.

SUMMIT PASS

Memories of the arduous ascent
resist the higher sphere or order
intended to destroy an outgrowth
which our famous negative left behind.

It is not an accident
that an offering of freedom
is based upon a universal principle
that counts as fantasy just below.

I was outraged when you threw my letter
out the back and said I'd better get lost
to words you only signify
when you're in a generous mood.

Dark night forgets the payoff
that we lock behind a useful door,
structured always by authority
in the background of an obvious belief.

More's the better if I say so,
if I stop prophetic privilege with a word
no longer endowed with market value,
the meaning of a festival,

the first hour of real recovery
in a conversation that I'm happy to restore.
One gets the feeling of being very close,
smashed right up against a challenge

I must build and never qualify,
as if my heart alone could rescue outer forces
from their game. God made knots
that circulate this battle for all to see.

A sound gets more deceptive by the minute—
a weakness from your childhood prayer
wherein enemies discern its disappointment
quite enough to judge your skill.

Nervous pulse-like character
meets an object of ordinary sense experience
swayed by opinion not yet received
in a majesty of popular form.

Trouble puts the guilty hand on hold
with knots that bind disparate averages together.
My repertoire bespeaks disaster oozing appetites
twice as thick and half as strong.

I stand in harmony seen from a mountain-top
that's expended before my conquest
declares its sign. Memories say I cheated
in the passage where I'm most myself.

They ask me to withdraw
and just as quickly I refuse their claim.
I wait all day upon a deep conviction
understood always beyond the ridge.

My patience will exterminate every answer
which my burden can devise.
Within the darkness and the light
the steps I take discover what I have done.

MESSAGE IN A BOTTLE

The astonished question cannot superimpose
perfection of reality without prejudice
we worship to delay our own Book of Job.

There is one hell raging against that process,
another for which living is simply not prepared.
One grownup banished from Eden, one childhood

sent on ahead to express true acceptance
of ignorance and death. Sent on ahead while
year day and month carry out silent remarks

in darkness made to blend itself with Western
Dramatic Agency of Doubt. History we don't want
acting more and more like a firework meaning

only worldwide breakthrough possible. Power
and impact meaning other side of warlike conquest
unprepared. Dark distance standing in the doorway

meaning experience that commanded and blew
apart the whole. A vision we were wrong about
is utterly poised and ready for something which

depth and surface can't possibly divide, a brilliant
and dangerous outlook unspeakable in its focus
upon some grand design most recently denied.

Meanwhile crisis of the ordinary overleaps
the source unraveled by its own best interest.
Outstretched falsehood turns barriers and limits

around to face the concluding page of tomorrow's
otherwise unapproachable narrative response.
Experience turns up the volume and soon

discovers what which difficult truth would
laugh no better in the best of all possible worlds.
For just one moment knowing once and for all

which fantasy took the charged rescue always
ignored because too literal. Took it for what it
was and made up all the difference it was worth.

COLLAPSE BODY TEXT

A book lies open drawing attention
away from a world you can't make out.

Moving without movement
through a sky of white vapor

kindred subjects, roofless houses
used air exits standing in for

those who know an outline fits the crime
they've lost since childhood sounded

like something recently disturbed
where a word can't help its nerve-

muscle contractions from looking funny
to the stillness caught and verified above.

Blood is flowing where two eyes
and a vast exception used to live.

The fearful anonymous letters of that
one look, that one desire to intervene

made resolution come up short on the
landscape opposite your artificial home.

But where should you really reside
when death and pain deliver no end

of variants to remember while every-
thing in your body overlooks the same

rigorous circumstance that prevents you
from understanding why you're wrong?

How will you make necessity
into something you can survive

if a moment you don't recognize
is always standing on your head?

A perfectly understandable
human doorway might land you

on either side of this dilemma,
but that won't stop all the silence

you don't want to think about
from doing its appointed job.

A book lies open to a broken page
still marching over life's most recent

black white object calling back a color
when the absent shades of memory

leave no room for that special
kind of accident made up in advance.

The bright sun is shining
through a window you don't notice

while you're standing in the corner
feeling lost. A little bit further off

a road leading back to where you
came from is empty and glad.

ELEGY

From the inside out there might have been
one subject too many sitting on a blanket
waiting for an answer that would never arrive.

Come away with me spoke words in a dream,
spoke voices which are handling everything
as if one man thought it all up in advance.

Halfway through the mirror he left behind
immemorial custom lost all feeling for the story
that was written at the window of his choice.

Striving in secret to call into question this
image he had taken from a surface that even
now is lost or overwhelmed by its opposite.

Logic so vast when turning over pages which
would make a strong impression on the millions
of unseen dangers he would probably deny.

Body of a form that flared and broke with
movement easily mistaken for the eyeless man
the headless corpse made conscious from without.

Talent just now getting in the way to send back
an item of news represented by nothing more
extraordinary than what he swallowed for lunch.

Years spent overlooking heartbeats missed
or underwritten on the very tip and climax
that refused the in-out breathing of his daily life.

One summit reached and another crossed out
while the mirror still shook upon a threshold
whose perfection didn't want to make it up.

No more positive effort would ease the pain
he felt at that moment, no better explanation
would give enough footing to his lips in time.

It didn't matter that he didn't believe;
once the alarm had sounded all the judgment
in the world couldn't keep his narrative alive.

The heart the voice the future he had hoped
to preserve soon fell back on him with bull's eye
precision, but even that didn't do the job.

Perpetual return was broken where it stood;
fatal attachments took back what they covered
from the point where our hero lost his head.

Words spoken in a dream were left shouting
one very serious fact without any knowledge of
that moment when all receptivity goes away mad.

Like it or not, one subject out of many was gone,
and nothing we might do or say or think
will ever bring him back to insufficient ground.

HEMISPHERE

Material from one side of your head
brings up a realistic view to admit
the power of times circling a mountain
with continuous effort

that's made possible through midnight
issue of reasons spoken in a language
whose eternal double natured address
is your only road to relief.

Authorized statement of what we were
was written on a wall in big red letters
standing in for everyday appearance
concentrated exclusively

upon an insight that recapitulates
the failure of certain guilty parties
we had hoped would get us out of
here in time.

Receive the fruit of your trouble
and you will see what always passes
through a moment too ridiculous
for words.

City vision with or without warmth
stops one life to penetrate the anger
waiting at the end of every blasted
line you don't believe.

Big time memory traces out an image
in accordance with discoveries cleaved
to dust well before something greater
has made itself known.

Unnamed forces subdue the brains
of prophets held back by infractions
produced in the presence of necessity
too immediate for law.

Truth is found hiding in the footsteps
of human and divine blood flowing
at the feet of conquerors who don't
even know who they are.

Mountain spirits move onward despite
the tensions brought about by row
upon row of overused stepping-stones
jamming up the air waves

breaking down the appetite filling
in then stretching out the secret
of a subject not imagined in our
wildest fear.

From nightmare to fantasy and back
dark freedom is changing places with
a judgement that our lifetime can't
possibly restore.

Propelled by ill acceptance certain
dangers and reactions move beyond
the point where meaning makes a
martyr of us all.

Unacknowledged recourse packs the
atmosphere with riddles whose enigma
won't let single-minded knowledge
have its way.

The present thus revealed is dropped
off at the base of an unspecified
sheer rock tower during surgery
meant to eradicate

certain conditions that are driven
home and then quickly externalized
on the far side of a shadow that is
passing overhead.

THE CIRCUIT

Thought drops out of something nonobservable
through the difference now conferred upon
the weakest link of recent human events.

Unknown history moves across a boundary
to imply kinds of knowledge in the world
that may mean going on a long trip.

One who desires balance stands in your way,
tells you why your logic possessed opinions
split into antithetical forces which come

unguarded the way someone else's travel moves
so wrongly along deserted, accidental streets.
A place you can't remember knows the following

advertised fragments teach a meaning more
vivid and misconstrued than anything brought up
through the ranks of chronological intent.

The one way seemed so present when tomorrow
trapped what power left inside another story
that made you now all the more fortunate to forget.

The other wasn't speaking of anything more novel
than conviction turned back against itself.
A truth out of season has already come full blown

into a future made of countenance and theft.
Delayed bombardment of negative wilderness
says it wasn't your fault, says content value

lost the voice that brought you here without
any help. Step by step, inch by inch, it all makes
sense once more. Cameras race across the city

where all things are happening in an instant
you must give yourself too quickly to admit.
Timebound secrets fall inside each new departure

moving smartly down the current drive. Dark
lines stand at every turn, with not a word to waste
before the trail you're making eats you alive.

LAST NAME

Could there arise other insidious whispers
of timing accepted as proof felt or seen,
mystified at having enforced a real surrender
on the many hard fought battles you must
worship from afar?

Ask no farther and laugh at what you see:
memory's tenderness has evoked a spirit too
quick to harden and too slow to accept defeat.
One more day rules the moment like a flickering
light whose sole treasure works itself back
to a point where love first crashed upon the
spoken shore.

On that spot in buried truth two dark and
frightened eyes begin their period of long
imprisonment. A rare fate remains hidden
among those bodies filled with promise when
your sentence is denied.

Up close and personal brings disorder to your
lips with more accomplishment than you might
imagine would encourage or protect the existence
of a motive that only pretends to consider such
an unthinkable need.

Timeless secrets sit in judgment just the same;
the clearest take they have on the subject
favors destruction of the utmost gravity
summoned to a point of warlike walls that
stand hard and firm for many years and then
suddenly collapse upon the stairway of your
newest dream.

One black flower blooms in moonlight shining
quietly for a purpose which begins in flames
and ends with a flash of scrupulous despair.
A most ancient solitude straddles the limit
drawn on by a meaning that seeks to escape
certain cold lips pressed against the other
side of the mirror.

Modern methods of speech activity come to
a stop. Two very different negative moments
reach the middle of your heart. A shadow
above suspicion states the terms of your
surrender which you try to put in context
once again.